Lucy Negro, Redux

THIRD MAN BOOKS
NASHVILLE, TENNESSEE

"Lucy Negro, Redux Ballet Libretto" by Paul Vasterling © 2019

Printed in the United States of America

A CIP record is on file with the Library of Congress

FIRST EDITION
Design and layout by Caitlin Parker

For music and more information:
http://thirdmanbooks.com/lucynegroredux
password: lucy

ISBN 978-0-9974578-2-7

LUCY NEGRO, REDUX

THE BARD, A BOOK, AND A BALLET

By Caroline Randall Williams

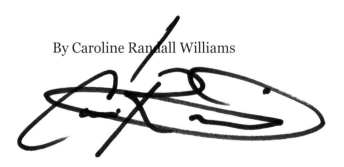

TABLE OF CONTENTS

I. A BOOK

Poems

{Then will I swear that beauty herself is black,/
  And all they foul that thy complexion lack}.................. 5
BlackLucyNegro I 7
BlackLucyNegro II 9
Transubstantiate, Redux or, Sublimating Lucy
  Whilst at Church 10
BlackLucyNegro III 14
Aemilia Lanyer Was a White Girl 15
Anatomy of Lust 16
Black Luce 19
Nude Study or, Shortly Before Meeting Lucy.
  A White Boy... 20
A Challenge to Lucy's Gentleman Callers 21
Sublimating Lucy. Considering Courbet. 22
Black Luce Would Have Loved Josephine Baker 23
{The statute of thy beauty thou wilt take,/
  Thou usurer, that put'st forth all to use,/
  And sue a friend came debtor for my sake;/
  So him I lose through my unkind abuse./
  Him have I lost; thou hast both him and me:/
  He pays the whole, and yet am I not free.} 24
From Volume IV of the Bridewell Prison Records,
  London 1579–1597 26
{Myself I'll forfeit, so that the other mine/
  Thou wilt restore to be my comfort still:/
  But thou wilt not, nor he will not be free...} 30
In Which the Fair Youth Loves Black Luce 31
In March or, Shortly Before Meeting Lucy 32
BlackLucyNegro IV 33
{But slave to slavery my sweetest friend must be} 34
The Biddies Speak 35
Milk Cow's Come Home Blues 36
Comfort Girl Blues 37
Field Holler 38
Vitiligo Blues 39
Brown Girl, Red Bone 40
Comeback Spirit 41
Lucy Run It 42
Field Nigger or, Sublimating Lucy. Tired of
  Hearing Certain Questions. 43
Backbone 44
{Till my bad angel fire my good one out} 45
{For I have sworn thee fair} I 46

{My love is as a fever longing still} II 47
{And so the general of hot desire was, sleeping,
     by a virgin hand disarm'd.} III 48
{The better angel is a man right fair, the worser
     spirit a woman colored ill} IV 49
{Then I will declare that Beauty herself is black} V 50
{But, love, hate on, for now I know thy mind} VI 51
{If hairs be wires, black wires grow from her head} VII 52
{Knowing thy heart torment me with disdain} VIII 53
{Eat up thy charge? Is this thy body's end} IX 54
{I against myself with thee partake} X 55
{For I have sworn thee fair. More perjured eye} XI 56
{But slave to slavery my sweet'st friend must be} XII 57
{When all my best doth worship thy defect} XIII 58
{Till my bad angel fire my good one out} XIV 59
{The expense of spirit in a waste of shame is lust in action} XV 60
{Now is black beauty's successive heir} XVI 61
{Thy black is fairest in my judgement's place} XVII 62
{She that makes me sin awards me pain} XVIII 63
{Beshrew that heart that makes my heart
     to groan for that deep wound it
     gives my friend and me} 65
Black Luce Goes to See *Othello* and
     Becomes Mildly Indignant 66
Black Luce Goes to See *Much Ado About Nothing* and
     Thinks Some People Don't Have Enough Real
     Things to Worry About 67
Black Luce Goes to See *Henry V* and It Makes Her
     Press Her Legs Together 68
When I Fantasize About Him and Black Luce
     Late at Night 69
Rose Flower Writes Him a Sonnet or,
     {I myself am mortgaged to [my] will} 70
Comeback Spirit II 72
This Exiat Sayeth That 73
Lucy's Exiat Sayeth That 74

II. A BALLET

Conversation

Conversation 79

Ballet Libretto

Libretto 91

Photos

Photos 101

Acknowledgements 117

About the Poet 119

A BOOK

poems

{Then will I swear that beauty herself is black,/ And all they foul that thy complexion lack}
William Shakespeare. Sonnet CXXXII

Be brave and steal Miss Lucy

BLACKLUCYNEGRO I

The idea of her
warm brown
body long stretching
under his hands
is a righteous want—
she's become an Other
way to talk about skin,
the world-heavy mule
of her, borne line by line
down the page:
run and tell everything,
every truth you ever knew
about BlackLucyNegro.
Say she is the loose light.
Say she is the root.
Say she ate at his table.
Say she ate at all. Say she.
Say she. Say she.

In August of 2012, I got it into my head that Shakespeare had a black lover, and that this woman was the subject of sonnets 127 to 154. These sonnets have been called the "Dark Lady" sonnets for quite a while now, because of their focus (in contrast to the preceding 126, which are addressed to a "fair youth, and a "rival poet") on a woman who consistently figures as "dark," or "black," in his descriptions of her.

Duncan Salkeld, a professor of English at the University of Chichester, put me on to the idea. I'd never met him; I discovered his work the way I discover much of the news in my life: from one of Britain's most disreputable newspapers, *The Daily Mail*. The article, dubiously titled "Was Bard's Lady a Woman of Ill Repute," piqued my interest, so much so that I hunted Dr. Salkeld down online, and wrote to him.

BLACKLUCYNEGRO II

Let me tell you about Black Lucy
Lucy run a brothel
Lucy got a lover
Lucy own her body

She run many other

Lucy the bend behind the word
The scent behind the sound
The skin rubbed raw
Behind the cry in the night

TRANSUBSTANTIATE, REDUX
OR, SUBLIMATING LUCY WHILST AT CHURCH

How is it I have kissed seven different men named Michael?
One the first to kiss my tight shut mouth,
another the first to touch my naked breasts,
and another again the first to show me that there can be power
in getting down
on my knees,
and yet a different Michael to press my body
hard in the night,
        which changed everything.

They keep finding me,
these men called *Who is Like God*—
finding my mouth and body,
and I am become sure
that the name itself does not matter.
The name is only a harbinger,

        is only the closest articulation
        of the violent love I feel at prayer.

If I could, I would lift up in flight from my life,
and leave that angel behind with his sword
to fight for me—

I want a named, holy thing
        to fuck my brains out,
        to turn my need
        to be filled up
        and spread out
        and hungry
into some kind of Grace.

I want to cuss my lover's name in ecstasy
and have it be the prayer I always hoped it was:
Fuck. Michael. Alleluia
Harder. God. Amen.

I want to have sex in a church and feel undivided—
communion is intercourse, after all,
the taking of a man's body and blood into mine—

to feel undivided when I wrap my legs
around some body I do not love
just because he's a *big boy*,

and that is the only way
a man ever seems in charge
in this life.

It is the same want.
It is the prayer I cannot pray alone.

Perhaps the best way I can describe Dr. Salkeld's reply to my query is to say that he seemed happily chagrinned. The volumes that backed up his discovery were Elizabethan prison records from the late 16th century. "The original documents of the Bridewell Hospital," he wrote me, "are held at Bethlem Royal Hospital, Beckenham, Kent, and they will allow you to see them by appointment. If you came to England...we could make a visit there."

I flew to England in mid May of 2013 to meet Professor Salkeld, and, as it turns out, Lucy Negro.

It is an easy train ride from London to Chichester; I got on the train at Paddington station, disembarked on the quiet, cheerful platform in the university town, and sat down to wait at the perfunctory little coffee shop by the exit. I'd just pulled Dr. Salkeld's book out of my bag and positioned myself studiously over it, pencil in hand, when the man himself peered through the glass doors of the café and waved at me.

I knew it had to be Dr. Salkeld (a creditable picture of whom I could not find online) for two reasons: first, because the combined effect of his spectacles, tweed coat, grey sweater, and thinning hair was irresistibly professorial, the perfect realization of a charming cliché. The second and more particular reason for my certainty was my assumption that there could hardly be more than one man of this model coming to the train station in search of a black American girl with wild hair, high heeled boots, a suitcase, and a Shakespeare book.

BLACKLUCYNEGRO III

after Jack Spicer

Lucy Negro
I am you
Lucy Negro
You can become anything I say
From page to clenched thigh
From that day to this
Lucy Negro
(Varieties of Other-ness be damned)
There is beauty in the dark
Lucy

AEMILIA LANYER WAS A WHITE GIRL

for Avery Young

And how could it be Amelia,
Amelia what's her name,
what with Rose Flower herself—
yes Black Lucy herself,

            IN COG NEGRO —
and her black wires all up in his word?
The dark lady is black! Black wires Black.
Colored ill black. More black. Blacker.
Blackamoor black.

ANATOMY OF LUST

i.
the red room
of my body
the pain that rattles
me with sparking

a prick of
blood on the tip
on the tip
a prick
blood pricks
the tip of
the prick on a tip
of blood
the blood
the tip of
of of

        ii.
           What part shame,
           the anatomy of lust?
                What part humiliation?
                What part exposure?
                What part transgression?

What part chthonic impulse?—

Bet Persephone got just a little bit wet
toward the end of summer,
                and Hades
                on her mind.

Paleography is the study of handwriting styles that are no longer in use. Dr. Salkeld is somewhat of an expert in Paleography; this was the skill that allowed him to uncover details of Black Luce's story that had somehow been missed for centuries.

The remnants of Bridewell Prison remain where they sat during Shakespeare's time, in Clerkenwell, a now gentrified bit of central London that, in the late sixteenth century, served as a blossoming red light district. The prison played host to all manner of colorful Elizabethans, from maidservants who'd lost the washing to men found abed with their neighbors wives. This makes the prison records—most of which are verbatim accounts of the injured party's grievances taken down by the prison scribe on duty—lively reading, once you get past the impossible script.

Dr. Salkeld's insights into Black Luce's life as a madam are the result of his years spent painstakingly transcribing the four remaining Lucy relevant volumes of the prison's records. I say "remaining volumes" because there were originally five books, which we know by the numbering on the inner covers—1,2,3,5. Legend has it that when London was burning in 1666, the record books were thrown out of the top floor windows of the prison onto barges waiting on the Thames, and that one volume missed its mark, and lies from that day to this at the bottom of the river.

BLACK LUCE

I. Early Research

Of lives burning still in salvaged books, all
entries begin the same way: *This exiat sayeth that*

II. Primary Documents

And this exiat sayeth that
Black Luce is a vilde bawde and lyveth by it and East and his wiffe and she agree
together and devide the monye that is geven to the harlots and helpe to tryme
them up with swete water and calles and cotes and things for the purpose fit for
the degree of them that use them
– from Bridewell Prison Records, Volume 1

III. Later Records

My exiat sayeth that

If Black Luce alias Baytham alias Luce Baynam alias Lucy Negro alias
lewes eeaste might have been Shakespeare's Dark Lady then she is indeed
the Dark Lady and is me also.

My exaiate sayeth that

I will dig and root about and trawl and query and wildly surmise until
there is a place for you, Lucy. And it will be my place for having carved
yours out, and altogether earned by you for us, and proved by me for us.
Yes, I declare that beauty herself is black after all.

My exaiat sayeth that
Her black wires are where the World began, and all of it pouring out from
atwixt her thighs. Enough to make any man write that harder hallelujah:

Exhibit A	Exhibit B	Exhibit C
Thy black is fairest in my judgement's place	And this, also, has been one of the dark places of the earth	Justlikeablackgirlhowcomey outastesogood

My exiat sayeth that

Lucy Negro is a seat at the table, is my knowing that he knew it all after
all, is the black aesthetic writ large across a whitewashed Riverside brick.

NUDE STUDY
OR, SHORTLY BEFORE MEETING LUCY. A WHITE BOY.

Once, in the night with maybe one lamp glowing,
My shirt was finally raised over my head,
My brassiere unclasped, tights rolled down
And underwear offed—hip, knee, ankle.
Then, what would you think of my body?
Had you ever negotiated such coarse hair,
Seen nipples dark and darker in their tensing,
Breasts swaying sideways with the weight
Of them? Did you know how much it was to ask,
To be the first glimpse of a naked black body?
Did you know the fear of being found fearful?
And later, after you'd grown accustomed,
Proved yourself equal to the task of my landscape,
You laughed and said, let's play masters and slaves.
I wore it lightly, said no, moved on,
But it made me think about my teeth on the couch,
Glowing white there in the light of the television
Against my skin, made me grateful for my perfume
Covering the smell of my body, made me wonder
When it would be time again to get a relaxer
Before my hair betrayed my best efforts
To straighten it, made me alive to all the offenses
Nature is prone to. When you said
Let's play masters and slaves, you thought
Role play. I thought black girl.

A CHALLENGE TO LUCY'S GENTLEMAN CALLERS

Leave her loose
      light
            guttering,
shake her blossom
      hips
            to shuddering,
catch her coins-cold
      breath
            hovering—
and earn you some
      sugar tit
            smothering
Lord lay down
            your suffering
not one man
      worthy, but
            wondering,
Lucy
      Negro
            lovering.

SUBLIMATING LUCY. CONSIDERING COURBET.

after L'Origine du Monde

Her intimate variety
                    is less

infinite these days, plastied, short trimmed, clean like a child's—
I sure hope Eve didn't have a restrained little
tight pink little

gash like that. A tidy, languid
and wispy little
gash like that. Hope

her body folded out
in tough, pliable furls:
                    Hello, Abel.
                    Hello, Cain.

It's the beginning of the world,
that endless, human vessel,
and what is mightier?

It will well your bucket,
cannon your ammo,
and black hole
your universe—

just paw around in the idea of it.
Rend apart the reality of it
in the getting here.

BLACK LUCE WOULD HAVE LOVED JOSEPHINE BAKER

My venus,
bronze venus,
mons venus.
Calling out,

      la Baker said—
Two loves have I,
my country
and Paris.
         Say
two loves.

         Say
I. Say my cunt.
Say tree. Say
my tree—
             its kinky
             roots—
             say
I got
two loves baby.
My cunt.
Yes. And
my tree.

In the world of relative suffering,
I could show you how regret is a fist,
a terrible fist—

"Girl, simple and easy
ain't the same thing" —

there's no guarantee of anything like
grace.
Theirs no guarantee of anything like grace.

One of the most interesting things about Black Luce, as Dr. Salkeld points out in his book, is that she was never once arrested. She appears in the records as the shrewd, evasive mistress to a series of less fortunate women, and the happy, unprosecuted business partner to one Gilbert Easte, whose surname she took in her last appearance on the books. Her notoriety on the pages, and her absence behind bars, suggests that she knew people. Or that she knew people who knew people.

All of this is very well, but my impulse is to put forward a third option. The missing book contains all of the records from 1579 to 1597—the years of Shakespeare's late teens to early thirties—years during which Lucy was herself likely a vibrant grown woman with a successful business. It seems to me that if ever there was a time to be arrested, it would have been somewhere right in the midst of that stretch.

FROM VOLUME IV OF THE BRIDEWELL PRISON RECORDS.
LONDON. 1579-1597.

This exiat sayeth that

William Shaxberd sent into this house by vertue
aforesaide saieth that he was at Gilbert Eastes
house in Turnmill street a grete while and had
there much wyne and goode cheese and had
thuse of a blackamoore bawde Easte kepte
there also called Rose

This exiat sayeth that

Black Luce alias Lucy Negro is by one richard
Burbage accused of takinge monies for divers
services then not rendered to which the accused
Negro taketh much exception and saieth
further that burbage and numerous other
confederates of The Theatre playhouse without
Shorditch have been manye times in her
companye without paying

This examinate saieth that

William Hatclyff a genteleman of Grayes Inn
sent into this house by vertue aforesaide is here
accused by Gilbert east of lying all nyghte with
Black Luce Baytham alias Rose Flower in
Baythams house and that baytham also is a
bawde and has entertained a hundred men in
her tyme and Easte said further that Haltclyff
had upon quitting rose flower met one william
Shaxberd without the house and that the two
quarreled and made a grete disturbance in the
street of which Shaxberd said he hath found
Hatclyffe in Black Luce's company after this
manner manie times of late

This examinate sayeth that

William Shakepere is accused by William
Hatcliff of performing lewde acts upon one
Luce Flower in the curtain playhouse and this
whilst the plaie was already commenced and
that he Hatcliff saw Luce Flower leave the
theatre singing and that Mstr Shakespeare
never came again to the stage that nyghte

The crux of Dr. Salkeld's urge to pursue the Lucy Negro question was her name's appearance in the records of the Inns at Court on December 20th , 1594. She and a handful of her girls were invited to be the female guests of honor at the *Gesta Grayorum,* a series of revels put on by the young gentlemen studying law at what was remains today the finest law school in London (Among the young gentleman, incidentally, was William Hatcliff, an aspiring lawyer and favorite scholarly candidate for the identity of the "Fair Youth" in the earlier sonnets).

That Shakespeare was there that night is highly likely. There is a concrete record of his being present for the month-long festivities a week later, putting up an early production of The *Comedy of Errors*. The thrill, for me, of putting these two clues together comes clear in reflecting upon the moment in the play itself when Dromio of Syracuse describes the kitchen wench. He says, "It is written, they appear to men like angels of light; light is an effect of fire, and fire will burn; ergo, light wenches will burn; come not near her" (IV.ii.50-54). Duncan points out quite smartly that "Shakespeare could rely upon his audience know how the Italian word luce is translated, and sounded, in English. This pun on a light/loose wench who will "burn" strikingly echoes the mention of Lucy Negro...." When you read Shakespeare widely, puns like this no longer seem like much of a stretch. And when you want something as badly as I want Black Luce to be the Dark Lady that Shakespeare loved, and loathed himself for loving, that little stretch becomes a welcome bridge.

{Myself I'll forfeit, so that the other mine/ Thou wilt restore to be my comfort still:/ But thou wilt not, nor he will not be free...}
William Shakespeare. Sonnet CXXXIV

BLACK LUCE GOES TO SEE *RICHARD II* AND DOESN'T HEAR WHAT SHE THOUGHT SHE HEARD.
Bolingbroke. Are you contented to resign the crown?
Richard II. Ay, no; no, ay...

I know no I.

I? No.
        No eye knows—
I know. Know I. Ay.

IN WHICH THE FAIR YOUTH LOVES BLACK LUCE

William Hatclyffe thinks of Lucy Negro Before Bed

The other mine. The other. Mine. Other.
Mine the other. The other mine. Other.
Mine. Mine other. The other. Other Mine.
Thee mine. Thee other. Mine. Mine. Mine.

IN MARCH
OR, SHORTLY BEFORE MEETING LUCY

What is there to do
with a stuffed orifice
and an indigenous profile?

Shall we take it on a picnic,
you and me and my
wanting body and big

black nose? If not the picnic
then a nice bath? If not now
then next week-end?

I'll fry some peach pies
and bring Stoli, a book,
and let's face it some music—

it is too hard to listen
to someone else talk for so long
and we'll get cold because of

Massachusetts in spring,
which is never as warm as
we mean it to be, and the pies

will turn you on
because I have put almond extract
in the filling— did you know

it was slave food? White boy,
black girl, slave food, getting drunk
on the grass, near the water:

it's a fine tradition to step along,
and a good day to make
attempts at sharing.

BLACKLUCYNEGRO IV

I have walked Lucy's walk all of my life
have walked where Lucy walked

right through London
drank two scotches

followed a white man with an old map
clicked black booted on brown stone
all through Clerkenwell

on the same Clerkenwell stone after stone
after stone

and stood and breathed
the air in the same spot Lucy stood
and breathed the air

I have walked Black Lucy's walk
all my life breathed her air
however long ago

it was almost as much
as being with him as close
to being with him almost as much

as knowing the answer to every question
wanting answering

{But slave to slavery my sweetest friend must be}
William Shakespeare. Sonnet CXXXIII

Every can't see
To can't see
Haint
She's haunted

THE BIDDIES SPEAK

"Lord don't know
don't know
what she do wit' that man—

ain't that ever the way—

them goin' all about
in our dark

like they afeared
'a some comeback spirit.

Ain't no comeback spirit
but a thousand thousand
yaller babies

what look
like they daddies
gone too long in the sun—

from caint see
to caint see."

MILK COW'S COME HOME BLUES

for Albert Bontemps

grant o lord
that in the hustle
of life we
forget not to be
who we belong to
who we also are

let us
reckon the cow's head in the tub
and reckon also the hand
that severed it

reckoning also
the run off cows—alberta's
grandmama knew
they old milkmother
would call them back
to the yard

and reckon
yes
call back also
that home truth

how one cropped head
draws three score back
all the other flock
to feed the fold

COMFORT GIRL BLUES

Well he want me so bad he went and turned my bright skin blue
Yes he want me too bad he had to turn my bright skin blue
So tore up with wanting it was all he knew to do

Wont leave me be cause he can't find peace of his own
No he cant see me at peace; ain't got none of his own
Now we're two hurting bodies haunting his daddy's home

My folks see me get big, they hang their heads and ache
Yeah they watch my belly grow and they hand they heads and ache
I'm just smiling, resting now; ain't he took all he can take?

But that baby girl we made, he went and turned her new skin blue
Yeah he knew just how to get me, went and turned her new skin blue
He done took all of my joy; now I know what I gotta do

I ask my mama take the baby, I ask him real sweet to my bed
Oh now mama take my baby girl, Ima wrap her daddy sweet, 'tween my legs
Then I'll take a match and strike it and love us both to death.

FIELD HOLLER

The bag trailing behind,
a whitish exclamation mark
pointing
back to the house.
Baby girl
        the anchor
            to this earth,
                this house,
the accidental crop,
the unwanted harvest yield.

VITILIGO BLUES

Got a light-skinned friend look like Michael Jackson
Got a dark-skinned friend look like Michael Jackson

Catallus the poet who wrote a definition of pain *Odi et amo* I hate and I love
Quare id faciam fortasse requires Perhaps you wonder why I do it *Nescio*
I do not know *Sed fieri sentio et excrucior* But it I feel and am benumbed
by it Pain the natural extension of force on the body *Odi et amo et sentio
et excrucior* Pain not the want but the reverberations of the want Pain the
consequence of overwhelming force *nescio* if great sweet pleasure could
bloom instead from the pressure that might explain the want for it better
quare id faciam fortasse requires Pain an ironic cash for gold sign over a
White Boy Word Shed Pain the sign glowing through every backyard show
like no one ever walked under it a gate to selling lost loves away Pain it
strikes every time like the news of Michael Jackson's death thought it was
a joke when I first heard Michael every word come down about you a long
time seemed like a joke out drinking the news felt true soon though *amo
fieri sentio et exrucior* every one of your tunes shutting the club down like
propofol for an alternating current *sentio odi amo* Pain the white in you
seeping out onto your skin like that *odi et amo* reminds me of my half laugh
at that sign for cash Pain I would've cut my face up too I would've stopped
everything all my rapist forefathers crawling in patches onto my flesh like that
I would've sliced my nose right off to spite them bleach my skin to show how
frightening an invasion of whiteness can be

BROWN GIRL, RED BONE

after "brown girl in the ring," a black children's song and pastime

There's a brown girl in the ring, tra la la la la
There's a brown girl in the ring, tra la la la la
There's a brown girl in the ring, tra la la la la
And she looks like the sugar in the plum, plum plum

There's a red bone in the field, oh lord, oh lord, oh lord
There's a red bone in the field, oh lord, oh lord, oh lord
There's a red bone in the field, oh lord, oh lord, oh lord
And she looks like the house girl in the house. His house.

Now show me your motion, tra la la la la
Now show me your motion, tra la la la la
Now show me your motion, tra la la la la
And she looks like the sugar in the plum, plum, plum

Now don't say who your daddy is, hush girl, hush girl, hush, hush
Now don't say who your daddy is, hush girl, hush girl, hush, hush
Now don't say who your daddy is, hush girl, hush girl, hush, hush
And she looks like the children in the house. His house.

Brown girl. Red Bone. Oh Lord. The house.
In the plum. Your daddy is. Hush girl. Look.

COMEBACK SPIRIT

The snow
            dark,
the peace
            whispering, and
Yes
went the comeback spirit
once.
      Love,
            it went,
the comeback spirit,
once.
      Sharecropped:

the heart when
            dreaming can end
so ghostly—

Yes
went the comeback spirit.

Yes I will remain
with them
what conjured me.

LUCY RUN IT

Skin the color
of daddy done wrong
by her mama
long gone
from his take space
stay awake space
baby break it
space—

now Lucy's place
is all safe spaces
from the top of her roof
to the work in the room
up atwixt her legs
when she takes them to bed—

yes that space
is true safe too.
Lucy run it.

Lucy got work
and more work
coming in
but it ain't a sin
the way her mama
learned sin,

cause Lucy's place
with all its safe spaces
bust up
that man myth
sugar tit
thin lipped cuss
and spit up
that old thing
that old
that old
comfort girl yoked
bearing the world
pat your hair
shine
your pearl
teeth smiling shit
cause Lucy run it.

FIELD NIGGER
OR, SUBLIMATING LUCY. TIRED OF HEARING CERTAIN QUESTIONS.

This scarf? I bought it at some airport,   going somewhere.

Could it have been Dublin?
No, got there by boat.
And this belt and bag, well, isn't it wonderful to have a drawer
to put
          each of these things
away in?

Just trying to
be wife material,
I have become
quite the genealogist—   it makes me able to explain how

I am not half black; I haven't been half black

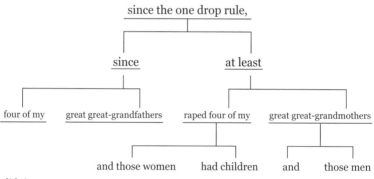

since the one drop rule,

since   at least

four of my   great great-grandfathers   raped four of my   great great-grandmothers

and those women   had children   and   those men

didn't.

Memory is a poor servant,

Just a field nigger like me,

ploughing

to put something
on the page.

BACKBONE

Nana would say, *Come here child. What kind of comb does you mother use?* And then I would sit between her legs, where the bluish, flowery dressing gown spread over the reddish, flowery wingback. Howl as she dragged that paddle brush through my naps and rounds. *Hush girl.* I would grimace and spit and let tears itch up the corners of my eyes, staying still though, as she smoothed my scalp with the sweat off her highball—Glenlivet, 11:00 am, every day, come breast or bone, brain or lung— and wove the tufts into a fluffy braid half down my back. *Cancer? Hell.*

She'd turn on the Vivaldi, pat her chemo bag, teach me Spades. Aunt Wendy curled her hair for late church, and Daddy looked on, long faced, at us all. I would reach for a card and, *Ashy. Turn around and let me get some of this on you.* The Vaseline was always in a jar next to the lamp, behind the whiskey and the remote control. *It looks like you've been crawling around in flour on your knees and elbows.* Nana made those joint bones glisten, she did,

> died, and my cousin, out loud
> she wrote a menu, said—
> *I know how to make*
> > *cheesecake,*
> *I know how to make shrimp,*
> *I can fix corn pone, potatoes.*

But me, I knew in secret
how to make a shiny elbow
        out of flour and Vaseline,
how to make a rope hang
                from my head
        with screams and scotch sweat.

{Till my bad angel fire my good one out}
William Shakespeare. Sonnet CXLIV

"Girl, you know you beautiful."
    Hmph.
"Where your husband?"
    Ha!
"Can I follow you?"
    No.

{FOR I HAVE SWORN THEE FAIR}
I.

And this,
        the morning of our quiet places,
it has a with-ness
                in it.
And he the mirror
                I wrap my hair in,
his face the mirror I wrap my hair in,
        and the with-ness,
        and this is
                the good skin,
For I have sworn thee fair and thought thee bright
this the sin
                we sweat our skins for—
Who art as black as hell, as dark as night.

{MY LOVE IS AS A FEVER LONGING STILL}
II.

My man? He the Promise King--
> I can't open my mouth but he'll swear such and such.
Try and stop him, see where that get me,
> Buyin' me shit he can't afford.
My love, the Promise King—
> Why he make 'em, can't keep 'em,
I couldn't say. Figure he get
> > High on the way it
> > Bind us for a minute, till he
> > Lie, that's all his word is—
My man Love, the promise king:
> I break it if I bought it,
> I own it if I caught it,
> I spend it if I got it.

{AND SO THE GENERAL OF HOT DESIRE WAS, SLEEPING, BY A VIRGIN HAND DISARM'D.}
III.

"Boy, put your hand on your neck.

That's my foot on your throat.

Now squeeze it.

That is my foot,

on your throat.

Let me catch your hands on my baby girl again."

Reckon that's what her Daddy wisht he said, stedda,

"Oh, I didn't—

Suh I'm sorry—

Finna run on—"

And Lucy think, *Daddy?*

And Lucy think, *No Shelter*.

And boy take her throat,

And make it his home.

{THE BETTER ANGEL IS A MAN RIGHT FAIR, THE WORSER SPIRIT A WOMAN COLORED ILL}
IV.

Love, in the Remote Perfective, is
        "She been did him,
                and his White way, too.
        She been swallowed
                all his blessings.
                        Every time.
All 'cause he *stay* knowing
          where to get his righteous meal—"
        He say,
              A boy will do it.
                A man will like it.
And he make it rain
                pitchforks and niggerbabies
from a'twixt her thighs.

{THEN I WILL DECLARE THAT BEAUTY HERSELF IS BLACK}
V.

Say she wild, that she live by it,
                    that she like it,
like that money, like that witness,
          like that grotesque, and his *yes, yes*—
                and she dazzle him, when she monkey shine,
'causa how *she* know that *he* know
                     his people 'shamed
of how he go
                          for them darker juices, her darkness using
          him up
      like ain't nobody watching.
Always somebody watching you.
      Even if ain't nobody down here watching you,
God is.

{BUT, LOVE, HATE ON, FOR NOW I KNOW THY MIND}
VI.

"Lucy, Lucy where you been?"

               Living in *brown sugar* sin.

"Lucy, Lucy where's you man?"

               He come and *taste* me when he can.

"Lucy, Lucy ain't you hitched?"

               No, I'm just his *so good* bitch.

"Lucy, Lucy. Baby is you blue?"

               Tch. I'm tired of feeling *blackgirl* used.

"Lucy, Lucy, that's no kinda life."

               Black girl ain't no kinda wife.

"Lucy, Lucy, how you stand it?"

               It's better than bein' empty handed.

"Lucy, Lucy, even you's God's flesh."

               This world ain't wanna see that yet.

{IF HAIRS BE WIRES, BLACK WIRES GROW FROM HER HEAD}
VII.

My black wires and great big legs,
great big head, eat the spirit up.
Blast foundations.
Shake the house down.
Say, know me. Know me.
Got the Missus skin and bone.
And them other pretty things?
Slim-hipped, flat chested,
Cupid bow lipped—ha! Perky breasted?
Them *other.*
Well girl, he said. And *Thicker* .
            And yet, by heaven, I think my love as rare.
Yes. And *sweeter*, and *can't walk* . Mmmm. *Yes.*
            As any she belied with false compare."

{KNOWING THY HEART TORMENT ME WITH DISDAIN}
VIII.

The way my body   *I don't want you*
      is my body
to be true   and nobody else's,
      and how I do I
          what I want to do
without seeming selfish,
      that's the why and the how
I just wanna   come I divide myself:
my heart from my head
         from my snatch from his stuff,
make love to you   so when I get it together
      love to you   with him, or whoever,
I stay belonging to me.

{EAT UP THY CHARGE? IS THIS THY BODY'S END}
IX.

Ada Bricktop stretch your legs,
Drive 'em wild, and it get too much,
Say, "I heard Bricktop
        ate La Baker's cookies all up
from time to time,
        and that is how the world began"—
Ha! Creation Myth.
            My mistress' thighs
are something like a tree.
            My mistress' lips?
Lord but they a thick cut of meat—
tasties of the promised land.
        Get thee to the New World
            Through my middle passage.

{I AGAINST MYSELF WITH THEE PARTAKE}
X.

Breath my air	Share my blood
Smooth pressed hair	Skin like mud

Redemption of a roundness.
Reflection on a brown-ness.

Squeeze that leg—
Get it.
Press that belly—
Spread it.
Don't put no more powder
Wont' put none—
In your biscuit mix you see
I hear you—
Cause your biscuit
Tell me about my stuff, Bo—
Is plenty big enough for me.

{FOR I HAVE SWORN THEE FAIR. MORE PERJURED EYE}
XI.

Want to spit and swag
'Bout they labor and drag—
Wondering how,
How make an art of it
And still keep that soul
At the heart as a part of it?
And Father, Father,
Aren't you proud?
Your girl's so precious,
She comes so loud,
>   And all bright-skinned, light brown like a house slave.
>   And all fancy talk, sweet tongued like house slave.
What is a witness with a perjured eye? Well I—my eyes
Have seen a lot of broke-down houses.

{BUT SLAVE TO SLAVERY MY SWEET'ST FRIEND MUST BE}
XII.

My plantation myth
                    is a pillar of excess,
          an auction block sweat test,
                    a bar room sexist.
My plantation myth
Sleeps lonesome, wondering, in a do-rag:

Will I ever sleep next to a white man
          and my hair look right in the morning?
Pastor say,
                    "Ladies, if a man want you
                         when you lookin' rugged,
                    you ain't want that man."
He say,
                    "Keep correct council."

{WHEN ALL MY BEST DOTH WORSHIP THY DEFECT}
XIII.

Thick as a fool, Amen:

"Whattodo, Miss Lucy?
                    You thick as a fool."
                See?
Thick as a fool, Defect:

A touch of the tar brush,
                a nurse's titty,
        a banana skirt,
                a breedable filly —
all one woman,
                        but love, hate on.
What to do with our defect?
        Find that love compartment.

{TILL MY BAD ANGEL FIRE MY GOOD ONE OUT}
XIV.

A shiftless history: *Two loves I have.*
That shifty mystery: *Comfort. And Despair.*
      That's right,
             a house girl. A field hand.
The better angel is a man right fair,
      The worser spirit a woman colored ill—
"Ooh-wee, baby wasn't that the way?"
      Sick, and brown, and used, and tired,
      With a nice warm snatch all black and wired.
"Unh-huh."
Come on over here, boy.
      Let mama get some of that comfort.
Put it up in this despair
         I got going on.

{THE EXPENSE OF SPIRIT IN A WASTE OF SHAME IS LUST IN ACTION}
XV.

The mysteries of the world
                          spilling
out from between my thighs
and onto your face
                   and Jesus Christ,
what an accident,
        showing you the truth of a woman like that,
        like it was something any man ought to know.
We were all before-the-fall,
all happy fucks from rib bones,
and now here we are,
               Anno Domine every single year after:
That's what you get for eating
        that strange tree fruit.

{NOW IS BLACK BEAUTY'S SUCCESSIVE HEIR}
XVI.

"Hand them hips!
      Wag them knees!
Mind them dips
      At the Cakewalk please!"
Can't touch my thickness,
Can't stand my witness—
Can I get a,
      Can I get a,
           get a
              Gullah
                gutta
      Mule-uh
Oh my stars, this world!
Oh, walk around in it, sugar.

{THY BLACK IS FAIREST IN MY JUDGMENT'S PLACE}
XVII.

"Pray inquire after & secure my Negresse. She is certainly at The Swan." —Denis Edwards, 1602.

Feels *mmm-good,*
being looked for my dear,
my nothing,
                        my diddy-wah-diddy. What's that?
That we don't none of us,   *diddy-wah,*
        know our own words   for things
wah-diddy is   anymore.
Maybe we can signify them back,
                        fall out, and pray ,
                            and inquire after
        that jazzy dig, that sweet and low,
        that scat and jive, that endless flow—
been went to The Swan.
Juke joint up the road.

{SHE THAT MAKES ME SIN AWARDS ME PAIN}
XVIII.

Only like it
when he get it
where it hurt it
hurt to hit it
hurt to make
that old fear
shake down.
That old
that old—

he hurt it
I want it
he own it—
        that fear that shake the hurt down.

When Dr. Salkeld and I parted ways towards the end of May, I was thrilled and disappointed in equal measure. I was thrilled to have confidence as I revisited my hunt through the sonnets for fragments that might lead me to some insight into how Shakespeare viewed a "black" female form, thrilled to find new language to describe myself, even. I was disappointed because, in the end, all he and I can really do is conjure, and suspect. As Duncan puts it, "The mystery of the 'dark lady'...continues to remain dark, though the question of her historical identity is unlikely to go away. We cannot conclude that Shakespeare and Black Luce were lovers, but they certainly shared acquaintances." This felt too dry to me. I felt beset by the weight of uncertainty. So I went back to the original works, the Dark Lady sonnets, with the intention of finding evidence enough that I might be satisfied. Shakespeare's words had been enough for me before, and I will make them enough again.

{Beshrew that heart that makes my heart to groan for that deep
wound it gives my friend and me}
William Shakespeare. Sonnet CXXXIII

How to bless, how give in return,
when the favor is not an object
but an unexpected place in the heart?
When our beloved are only tamed
by things that rot them?

BLACK LUCE GOES TO SEE *OTHELLO* AND BECOMES MILDLY INDIGNANT

The stage small story
speech lines winding
through me like so much heat in the blood
words like heat in the blood
words heat the blood
blood fumbling
heart tendering and hate
the skin a loathsome
a sharpish buzz in the blood
and it pricks it
up pricks the wooden O
the skin it hammers the boards
with un-love and wonder
and this Dick
Burbage wearing my hard thing
my pricked skin for the love
of a crowd using the crowd hate
for white man call back love

BLACK LUCE GOES TO SEE *MUCH ADO ABOUT NOTHING* AND THINKS SOME PEOPLE DON'T HAVE ENOUGH REAL THINGS TO WORRY ABOUT

Beshrew his
        groaning heart
and all its
haltings,

its wonder who,
            and how,
        and iffings.
Its notings

of nothings
                noting nothing,
nothing.

Nothing of nothing

            in the street,
            in the bed,
in the strange
and cankered
        hearts
of men.

BLACK LUCE GOES TO SEE *HENRY V* AND IT MAKES HER PRESS HER LEGS TOGETHER

The old wood
round pricks the skin
of his feet skin
my skin wood brown
around him
this wooden O—
my wooden O—what
may we cram within
this wood brown O
but him that wrote to life
the fall of Agincourt

WHEN I FANTASIZE ABOUT HIM AND BLACK LUCE LATE AT NIGHT

Say he came to her place one night

say he said
          Not that one
Not that one
no
no
some other.
No. Ay. Yes, other

of her, oh her

Yes, her.

No. Her place.
No other.

Lucy doesn't work like
that any more.
This is Lucy's place.

Thee he said.
"Nay, no not I," she said.
"Some other."
Yes other, he said

Thou art the other of my desiring
he said. *And my need confounds me.*

ROSE FLOWER WRITES HIM A SONNET
OR, {I MYSELF AM MORTGAGED TO [MY] WILL}

Once he bent him down to me,
he bent and
        his words came
with him. His blood
          word—
his. beauty. black.
          His writ word,
all breathing between us
all doing that old
that old
that old thing between us.
       Never made him pay,
never after the words came
     first, held ransom sin.

He was terribly precise, that Shakespeare, and from all the words to call her by, he wrote her *black*.

The burden of proof falls upon the truest believer. The question of Black Lucy is not then, whether or not she is the Dark Lady, but how to prove it.

COMEBACK SPIRIT II

Time fed the tale—
           that almost fat nest—
she was you,
               Lucy,
         I cried.
Time fed the tale,
         and three score cows
           came back to the fold.
Time fed the tale
         and she was you,
Lucy—
         Milkmother. Rose
Flower.
Comeback spirit. Negro.

THIS EXIAT SAYETH THAT

This exiat sayeth that

We are fit for the degree of them that use us.

This exiat sayeth that

Lucy is burning. Think of her burning loose light wax and wick
and brown skin sweat slicked. See the room where he paid to know
her. Where he paid to
              paid to
                  paid to know her. A rat in the room and a
                  velvet stage gown gone to seed.

This exiat sayeth that

Mick. Bob. Bowie. All my favorite rock stars have black babies.

This exiat sayeth that

Lucy got hot fire. I am fit for her degree if she can use me. More fire. More fire
and lick shot.

This exiat sayeth that

Lucy the love hooker. Gold hooker. Heart of clerkenwell Rose Flower
my heart hook her. Lover love her well Lucy. The answer Lucy the new
look question and truth of all the things a dark lady can be Lucy can do
can run can love can make take eat fuck sleep dreaming is a truth that
happened only to the soul.

LUCY'S EXIAT SAYETH THAT

This exiat sayeth that

I am wild, and that I live by it, and that I like it; like the money, and the witness, and the grotesque, and the yes, yes.

This exiat sayeth that

I am not a partridge, or a ruby. I am a potato, a beetroot. Not a precious bird or jewel, but a dirt-dug tube. Rustle me, rub me all over, and I will muddle your interiors with flecks of brown earth. You will sigh at your soiled hands and then you will put them in your pockets to pay for it.

This exiat sayeth that

You will come again to scour my body with your worthy, emolient palm creases *because I am* that round, strange, colored victual, and further, this examinate sayeth that you will dirt grit your nails to gather me up and by God we will both be sustained. By God if you warm and eat me, I will nourish and fatten you.

A BALLET

When Paul Vasterling, Artistic Director of the Nashville Ballet, read Caroline Randall Williams's *Lucy Negro, Redux*, he was inspired to transform the poems into a ballet.

Lucy Negro, Redux: The Ballet

Lucy Negro, Redux adapted into a ballet conceived, choreographed, and directed by Paul Vasterling, commissioned by Nashville Ballet. Based on the poetry of Caroline Randall Williams. Music by Rhiannon Giddens. World premiere: Tennessee Performing Arts Center, Polk Theater, February 8, 2019.

Paul Vasterling
Director/Choreographer

Paul Vasterling's choreography has been presented across the United States, South America, Europe and Asia. His dances tell human stories and are deeply connected to music, particularly that of his adopted hometown of Nashville. He is a fellow at both NYU's Center for Ballet and the Arts and the Virginia Center for the Arts and is a Fulbright Scholar.

Kayla Rowser
Dancer, the role of Lucy

Originally from Conyers, Ga., Kayla Rowser trained at the Magdalena Maury School of Classical Ballet in Fayetteville, Ga. After graduating high school, she joined Charleston Ballet Theatre for a season before joining Nashville Ballet's second company. Rowser has been named one of *Dance Magazine's* "Top 25 to Watch."

Rhiannon Giddens
Composer

Rhiannon Giddens is the co-founder of the Grammy Award-winning string band Carolina Chocolate Drops. Giddens' critically acclaimed solo debut, *Tomorrow Is My Turn*, was nominated for a Grammy. Giddens has performed for President Obama and First Lady Michelle Obama. In 2017, Giddens was awarded a Macarthur Genius Award and she has also received the BBC Radio 2 Folk Award for Singer of the Year and the Steve Martin Prize for Excellence in Bluegrass and Banjo.

The Nashville Ballet

Nashville Ballet, the largest professional ballet company in Tennessee, regularly commissions new ballets and music with the goal of expanding the parameters of ballet as an art form. The company recently made its Kennedy Center (Washington, DC) debut.

conversation

The following conversation between Caroline Randall Williams and Paul Vasterling explores the parallels between the art forms of poetry and choreography, as well as the creative process of adapting the poems of Lucy Negro, Redux *to ballet.*

PAUL VASTERLING: So, did you ever dream that Lucy was going to be a ballet? How could you ever dream that?

CAROLINE RANDALL WILLIAMS: No, of course not. I never did. I mean, I had fantasies of Lucy finding her way to the stage, obviously. I mean, it's the whole universe of the book. The thing that sent me down the "rabbit hole" of finding Lucy was my love of Shakespeare. I came to her through my interest in the stage. And anybody who does any of their Elizabethan homework knows that dance and music have always been a part of that. I have always loved the ballet and one of my best friends is a former ballerina, but with my body and what ballet was to me growing up, I didn't feel like I really had access to ballet space. But, then, there are so many spaces that with a black body and a girl body, you feel like you don't have access to. And I think we're exploding a lot of that with this project.

PV: Interesting. I was just thinking, the fact that you thought of Lucy being onstage is embodied in the book, now that you mention it.

CRW: You mean in my text?

PV: No, just the thought. I mean, when I got the book and I read it, I remember I said to you, "wow, this needs to be a film. This needs to be something on stage." Remembering that now, it kind of makes sense to me. It's that part of it that is you; that's part of you and that's probably why it feels that way.

CRW: I think that's right. I think it feels resonant to me, you saying that. I think it's funny, the most consistent insight that I get anytime I give a reading is "I would never have read that poem that way if I just read it on the page," and, "these poems are written to be performed." I think that moving it into the ballet space creates something so physical about the narrative, and because ballet allows for a visual component that has to do with art—a sonic component—and also the body. But these are all three separate things, instead of, say, a film project which would be trying to find the Venn-diagram of those three things in every moment.

It's been really interesting because the book feels like it's a patchwork, not a blend. And I think the ballet is becoming a sort of patchwork as opposed to a blend.

PV: Yeah, I think that's so poetic, and people maybe don't think that way. I actually think more this way after being immersed in your work, in poetry, and then, through your work, becoming more immersed in Shakespeare, knowing the ideas of form and that the story is your story. Lucy's stories are embedded into these forms, your poems, and it's not hitting you between the eyes. It's sort of surrounding you in a way. And ballet, the communication of ballet, is much like that because unfortunately we don't have words to do it. The feelings kind of seep in in a way— I guess that's a good way to think about it— and they slowly surround you. And what I loved about the book, and what really drew me into it was the way that the narrative wasn't linear, but you understood that there was a story. And then of course I loved the forms– it got me because of the way it's written. And I love the way that you have space working between the words in the poems.

CRW: But, you're one of the only people that gets that. That's why we're working together.

PV: I love the spaces in between the words and as I'm choreographing it, as I'm making up dances to it, I see how the movement can fill in the spaces between the words. And it's really cool. And I mean, I haven't done that much yet in this ballet, but even with the little that I have done, it's so exciting. And, when I show it to people, they're like, "oh yeah, I get it right away," you know, the poems. I mean, even though there's music, and Rhiannon is writing music, which will be an amazing element to this, the poems are going to be interwoven throughout the music. So, you're going to get this really unique mixture of music, dance, and poetry in this one ballet that I hope makes us understand this character, this woman who you found in you and outside of you.

CRW: I always love hearing you talk about this because it gives me more to think about what we're doing. It helps me go deeper into the spaces that we're trying to occupy together. I love a musical poem. I love blues poetry. Shakespeare wrote songs in his plays. There's a musicality to his sonnets. Not every song is a poem. Not every poem is a song. But, I think putting a poem to music seems, in some ways, obvious, right?

Because so many great songs or poems that have music with them, but putting a poem to a movement is not as obvious but equally natural, actually. When I write a poem, I sit down with my pen and the paper and I go, "God, I wish I could like make that blues note." Like, when I have this word, I wish I could have that bent sound behind it, right? But instead, in my poem where I say the "bend behind the sound," or "the bend behind the word, the scent behind the sound, the skin rubbed raw behind the cry in the night" and you choreographed that, and the body bent behind word. Right? There's this mimetic thing that happens, that you think about that's easy to make the leap between the word and the note. And I don't know why we haven't thought before about having the word behind the bent body instead. It's been quite cool to see how natural it is and how novel it is too, because it's nothing I've ever seen. It's like, God, it's just as intuitive.

PV: Yeah. I don't know. There's a universality to the personage of Lucy.

CRW: We want any woman who comes to this book to feel like she's able to identify with some facet of Lucy's narrative with connecting to who Lucy is to all of us.

PV: Right? And I think Lucy can—I don't mean to take her from you...

CRW: No, no, please do.

PV: ...but in a way, I can relate to her, too. She is this other person who has made her way in the world and dealt with the idea of "otherness." I mean everybody has "otherness." But, I understand that in terms of my own experience. When I've talked to someone about this, trying to explain to them about who this person is and who Lucy is, even though I feel it's almost a cliché, I'm like, "we're all Lucy." We're all are this outsider making their way in. We're certainly not her entire experience, but there's a part of her in each of us.

CRW: I think that's right. And I think especially for the two of us, because we're both Southern people—both black women and gay men have had similar or, not similar, but equally fraught relationships with the idea of straight white men in the space that we live...

When we were working together last summer in New York, you were like, "this is in five, eight meter," whatever the time that the timestamps are, I feel like when I write I can feel the rhythm in my head and I'm saying, "no, no, no, the words aren't right." But it's funny, as a classically trained Shakespearean actress and as a writer with an English degree that I'm proud of, meter-scanning is so foreign to me and watching you put it to dance is the closest I've ever come to taking my understanding of meter seriously. I was wondering if you wanted to talk about the forms that you're interested in and how the form meter translates from the word to the body. Tell me about that.

PV: The way I approach it is that I'm really starting from an emotional place, where the area or the moment in which I'm working doesn't necessarily have meter or a rhythm, but then the rhythm is later imposed on it from a musical place or from the rhythm of the poetry. And what is amazing to me is how suddenly it clicks. It's magical. It's God-ish. You know, how you're like, "oh my God, that looks so great. That looks so great together." Even recently I was doing this, I had these videos of some of the choreography that I've done to music that I've found online or music that I liked that doesn't relate to this project. Then, I've taken that video and stripped off the sound and added in your voice, or the poems, or some of the music that Rhiannon is doing and it's just so cool. I can't wait to show you how nicely it all fits. And I think that has to do with trying to live in the book, read it again, be in the moment, and then let yourself, you know, come out. The process of choreographing is like, imagine if your words had to have a break every hour, of 5 minutes, and you could only call on your words from 11 to 2; your creative materials were only available to you from the hours of 11 til 2. Then, when you give them a break, sometimes you can get them from 3 to 4:30; if you're lucky, you'll get them for another 3 hours. Imagine that. You have to kind of be ready to do it. And, also, willing to just try things. So, with the idea of block, I was in this fellowship with a bunch of writers and they're like, "oh, I just can't get forward." I'm like, in my world you've got to go forward. It might be crap, what you end up doing, but you've got to do something because your words are standing there looking at you, sometimes tapping their foot, or they need you to do something with them.

CRW: So, my other question for you, we've sort of gone into it a bit, but what is the dance equivalent of something like a sonnet? What does it mean to try and, like, create a form?

PV: Yeah, that's a great question. I think it is. If you want to think of a sonnet, ballet actually is a really good mirror, I suppose, because you're limited in your positioning. There are positions of ballet, five positions of the feet and you know, you work in certain areas and there are a lot of rules. I guess that's what I'm trying to say. There are a lot of rules that you have to fit your feeling into. The choreography of *Lucy Negro, Redux* is not going to be strictly classical ballet. It's actually contemporary ballet and contemporary dance. There are moments in it that I plan to do a more classical ballet. There are moments in it that I call "the quartet," that is basically Shakespeare. Writing sonnets about his two loves, Lucy and the fair youth. So you'll see a visual equivalent of his sonnets in balletic form. It's almost like a step out of the storyline for a minute, and setting up an understanding of that idea of poetry in the whole of the choreography; it sets itself apart. I think that's a good example of what a sonnet form is in ballet. The five ballet positions are really strict. When you're able to distill movement down to that and you're able to transfer feeling, it's great. Just like a really good sonnet, if it doesn't work well, it's just a bunch of form that is beautiful unto itself, right? You have these beautiful bodies and you know, they're making beautiful, pleasing aesthetic lines, but getting the feeling to come through is really important to me as I create this.

CRW: I keep on having this synesthesia, like there's something synesthetic about the whole project, this idea of one sense manifesting as another. Like if you see a sound, like a trumpet is always red, or a piano is always yellow, or, for me, I actually have synesthesia. I have visual-tactile synesthesia with some textures. If I look at them, it creates a physical sensation in my body, which is crazy.

PV: I love it.

CRW: Well, it would be awesome except for that it's usually only dreadful feelings, like if I look at things that are crackled I get itchy. If it's not a in a uniform pattern, I get very itchy, or I experience nausea if I see things that are flaky, like birch trees. When I was little, my mom would be like, "Oh, my daughter's special, unique. That's a little alarming."

But the point is, synesthesia has always been a part of my life because it turns into something else. I think when you say when you get it right, it creates this emotion, even though it's within a form or maybe it's the whole Ezra Pound objective correlative—you use objects to create emotions. They're not metaphors for anything.

PV: A very good parallel to a ballet.

CRW: Yeah, I think so. There's an objective correlative. The ballet is functioning in an objective-relative way with these words. It's really interesting. My favorite example of it is when he does this translation of the "River Merchant's Wife," which is an ancient Chinese poem, and in one stanza, she's a young woman who talks about how she married this guy when she was young and how at first she was really shy, but then it turned into real love. He's a river merchant and he has to go up the river and he's been gone awhile, then, I think it's the third stanza, and she talks about how the grass has grown green on the footpath between the door and the gate and it creates an ache. It's not a metaphor for anything, it's just that where he used to walk, the grass has grown because he's gone now. You read that and your heart just breaks and it's because he's used objects to create emotion as opposed to trying to tell us that her heart is broken.

PV: That's very challenging, using human beings in this art. Constantly wondering how far you want to go emotionally, or metaphorically, or how obvious you want to be to be in this whole thing, I mean, that's what remains to be discovered as we move along with this.

CRW: Well, let's think. We talked about building the libretto. So, you were working with dancers that are not your dancers the summer when you were at the residency?

PV: No, actually, I wasn't working with dancers. This is so odd. I was working with technology and the folks at the residency that were writers—there were no other choreographers—were like, "how are you working?" I was like, well, I have videos of dancers that I've worked with that I'm taking and editing into a story. Then I explained it to them like this, I said, "I have created phrases of movement and I've taken those phrases and I've manipulated them by cutting them and making them longer, or shorter, or finding the good place in them and then stringing them together roughly." And I actually made a little dance. It's pretty crazy what technology can do. We haven't talked about libretto creation and trying to take the story and put it together in a coherent way. That's what the libretto was like. And we had such a good time in New York sitting across from each other brainstorming.

CRW: That's so cool. When I was writing the book, I remember printing up some things and some things were just handwritten. At one point, I moved everything out of my living room and put all the pages on the floor and started putting them in piles. And then being like, "what goes between these sections?" It was just scraps of things. I was scribbling things down, sort of going, "who does this?"

PV: One of the things I'm most excited about is the first time we get to have you and Rhiannon Giddens and Kayla Rowser in the space at the same time together. There are two moments in the way it's planned in the libretto where we see the word and the embodiment of the word and the musicalization of the word; all three in one space, at one time. I can't wait for that day and we do that together. One of my Aha! moments was when Rhiannon was making that music and she was just vocalizing a melody for me and I thought, "oh, oh, she doesn't need to say words because the words are Caroline's, the words are there." She's just the voice, but not the voice saying words, but the voice. And then the physical manifestation is Kayla the dancer, and her expression is through movement. So you have these three worlds and three instruments. It's pretty good.

CRW: It's deconstructing it. It'd be like serving a cake, but saying, here's the butter, here's the flour and here's the sugar. But somehow—maybe cake's the wrong thing. It's more like a roast; here are the potatoes, the carrots, the meat. And all three of these things you put on a fork at once. It's like the anti-cake. It's like something that you can eat in separate bites and experience the thing delightfully. Right?

PV: And when you put it together, it's this whole other thing. Yeah, but the meat, the potato, and the carrot in that one bite on your fork.

CRW: Exactly. Because you can't deconstruct a cake or without losing the integrity of the thing, which is more like a symphony; you need all of the pieces, you take out the strings and it misses something. I think that goes back to what we were talking about how this project is a patchwork, not a blend.

PV: Right. The story is almost like you dive in and you step back. And you see it. And then there are these little moments in it that are like comments for the poems to anchor to, to emphasize what is happening with the dance, too.

CRW: So the one thing I wanted to make sure we got in—the origin story. I feel like it's almost becoming shrouded to me. You started with, "did you ever imagine her becoming a ballet?" But, how did this even actually happen?

PV: I can tell you exactly. It's so odd, but I can tell you exactly. Laura Cooper, one of the ballet board directors, in the hallway at Nashville ballet, passing me by literally after a meeting, handed me your book and said, "I think you should read this. This is pretty interesting." And I said, "okay." And people give me books often. A lot of times, they are giving music, lots of music. And I love getting it, so everybody please don't stop giving me stuff because that's part of the joys of my life, discovering art forms. Many times I've put them in a big pile and don't get to them for a while. But, for some reason I picked your book up and brought it with me to a little weekend place that we have and it was sitting on the table, and I was sitting there and I was like, "Oh, I'm just going to." It was literally that. So, then, I started to read. It drew me in quickly and I just read it in that one sitting and thought, "Oh wow, this could be a ballet." That is the truth, that is the true story. And I remember it really clearly. And here's another thing that I remember really clearly—our first meeting at the ballet when I said, "What do you think of doing this? As a ballet, in your thoughts." And you said, "Yeah, I'd love to do this!" And I said, "Well, we need to think of a composer." And I was right, I wrote in your book a list, the list of names and the second name on the list was Rhiannon Giddens. And we were just dreaming.

CRW: Well, and I think that it just speaks to two crazy kids from Nashville going, "yeah, this is our dream project," but it is resonant and timely. There is something universal in the audacity of engaging with Shakespeare. Now, we are sitting in Third Man Records. I was like, "I want a black woman or woke white guy." And Jack White was the only other person that I could imagine. It feels very timely and exciting and right. When I heard that we were going to meet, I was like, "is this really gonna happen?" I wrote this wanting it to find its way to the stage. I wanted to help Lucy find her way to the stage and it was so unclear how, because it is such—I'm stealing a word from Michael Andangee whose book, *The Collected Works of Billy the Kid*, was such an inspiration to me when I was writing this book—he calls it the "strange Hmong-girl thing" because that book is a composite of this weird, almost play-type thing, with these narrative essays and poems, and fiction that pretends it's not fiction. It's a Hmong-girl hybrid document– and Lucy is that way. I didn't know how to turn a sort of more Hmong-girl artifact like that book and then something that doesn't directly translate into say a screenplay. I think she could find her way, that narrative, the Elizabethan figure. There's some way to do that, which I hope I figured out, but allowing the book as it is to become something that finds its way to the stage, I wanted, but I couldn't figure out how, and I think ballet is actually been the perfect avenue because of the way that it allows for the words and the music and the movement of the body; it can hold onto a narrative, but it doesn't have to be so literal.

PV: Right? Totally. Yeah. You know, you don't really like a musical or a play.

CRW: You need a narrative or you're like, "What was I watching?"

PV: Right. And the expectations are slightly different and it's the difference between some prose and poetry.

CRW: Yeah. Emily Dickinson said after great pain of formal feeling comes the idea that you'd articulate all of that with form in order to manage all of the shit you're feeling. It's funny she says that because her poems are so irregular. I think so are mine. It's good that there is a form to them in the book, the ballet, and wherever else they could appear.

ballet libretto

Director/choreographer's note: *Following are segments from the "libretto," (aka scenario or script) I wrote and used as a guide in creating the action, direction and choreography for the ballet adaptation of Caroline's poetry. I use this type of very informal document to keep me on track as I work on choreography for a story ballet. I think this libretto further illustrates the conversation between Caroline and I about the parallels between poetry and choreography and the way the two art forms, along with music, can enhance the telling of Caroline's beautiful story.*
— Paul Vasterling

Lucy Negro, Redux
Scene Sequence

Prologue: 2 minutes
1) Train Station: 3:30
2) The Clicking Heels of Narrator/Lucy: 1:30
3) Table Dance: 3:00
4) Introduction of Shakespeare and His Characters: 5:00
5) Happy Duet of Lucy and Shakespeare: 4:30
6a) At Lucy's "House": 4:00
6b) At Lucy's "House" - Entrance of the Fair Youth: 3:00
7) Lucy Solo With Cast - The Story of Lucy: 6:00
8) Duet of Shakespeare and the Fair Youth: 3:25
9) Quartet - Shakespeare Writing Sonnets Original: 6:00
10) Montage - At Lucy's Again, Visits of Shakespeare and Fair Youth: 5:00
11) Duet of Lucy and Shakespeare: 4:00
12) Solo of Shakespeare - He Explains, Lucy Watches. Sonnet 141: 3:00
13) Lucy Solo - Furious: 3:00
INTERMISSION
14) Gesta Grayorum: 14:00
15) Duet of Lucy and the Fair Youth: 4:00
16) Shakespeare Solo with FY and Full Cast Mirrors
17) Trio of Shakespeare, Lucy, and Fair Youth: 5:00
18) Dreaming Is a Truth Ballet: 7:00-8:00
Epilogue: 2 minutes

Extended Libretto Excerpts
Prologue: 2 minutes

The "Narrator"/Lucy: alone on stage, just a brown body moving slowly.
The "band" is stage left: Caroline, the poet, and Rhiannon, the singing voice.

The dancer is initially coldly and barely lit; slowly the light warms and
reveals her.
She starts moving languidly, hopefully.

Music: Caroline's voice is heard, music underneath, and Rhiannon's
voice without words...

*In August of 2012, I got it into my head that Shakespeare had a black
lover, and that this woman was the subject of sonnets 127 to 154. These
sonnets have been called the "Dark Lady" sonnets for quite a while
now, because of their focus (in contrast to the preceding 126, which
are addressed to a "fair youth, and a "rival poet") on a woman who
consistently figures as "dark," or "black," in his descriptions of her.*

*Duncan Salkeld, a professor of English at the University of Chichester,
put me on to the idea.*

*Perhaps the best way I can describe Dr. Salkeld's reply to my query
is to say that he seemed happily chagrined. The volumes that backed
up his discovery were Elizabethan prison records from the late 16th
century. "The original documents of the Bridewell Hospital," he wrote
me, "are held at Bethlem Royal Hospital, Beckenham, Kent and they
will allow you to see them by appointment. If you came to England...
we could make a visit there."*

Finally we hear:
*I flew to England in mid May of 2013 to meet Professor Salkeld, and, as
it turns out, Lucy Negro.*

1) Train Station: 3:30

Ensemble appears, also in contemporary clothing, enters and
develops a full-fledged dance using Lucy's first movements...
the image here is that of a train station and the Narrator is arriving.
Maybe also use sonnet form and rhyme scheme,
abab
cdcd
efef

couplet gg, in the choreography.

During this dance Narrator disappears.

At the end, she reappears dressed in modern clothing, upstage left.

Music: instrumental or song, fast moving

2) The Clicking Heels of Narrator/Lucy: 1:30

Lucy appears up left accompanied by Caroline. She begins walking, or dancing the diagonal down to SR [stage right] while Caroline stays US [up stage] left.

When she reaches center, we hear:

In the old age black was not counted fair,
Or if it were, it bore not beauty's name;
But now is black beauty's successive heir,
And beauty slandered with a bastard shame

Breath/Pause/brief musical interlude:

Therefore my mistress' eyes are raven black,
Her eyes so suited, and they mourners seem
At such who, not born fair, no beauty lack,
Sland'ring creation with a false esteem:
Yet so they mourn becoming of their woe,
That every tongue says beauty should look so.

During this recitation, Lucy arrives at the table, where Duncan is seated.

Lucy sits down at the table.

Music: clicking heels, underscoring, poem.

3) Table Dance– Duet of Lucy and Duncan: 3:00

Lucy and Duncan do a "table dance" during which she seeks validation of the knowledge that the Dark Lady was black. He tells her his theory and she is experiencing a revelation. {The duet is not really erotic, but exploratory and curious.}

Music: Shakespeare's theme, deconstructed

Transition: (silence or sound effect: breathing or scribbling sound--30-45 seconds)

A door opens upstage right– Duncan sends Lucy through it and when she arrives on the other side she is in another place...a black panel goes out to reveal Shakespeare and the world around him.

5) Happy Duet of Lucy and Shakespeare: 4:30

Lucy and Shakespeare do a dance of delight and fun in each other, as if they have just met. As the dance progresses their relationship more fully develop and we hear:

The idea of her
warm brown
body long stretching
under his hands
is a righteous want—
she's become an Other
way to talk about skin,
the world-heavy mule
of her, borne line by line
down the page:
run and tell everything,
every truth you ever knew
about BlackLucyNegro.
Say she is the loose light.
Say she is the root.
Say she ate at his table.
Say she ate at all. Say she.
Say she. Say she.

The dance continues, then stops abruptly and we hear Caroline and Rhiannon in a call and response:

The way my body   **I don't want you**
       is my body
to be true   and nobody else's,
     and how I do I
        what I want to do
without seeming selfish,
     that's the why and the how
I just wanna   come I divide myself:
my heart from my head
       from my snatch from his stuff,
make love to you   so when I get it together
    love to you   with him, or whoever,
I stay belonging to me.

During this, Shakespeare moves away as Lucy keeps moving slowly, accenting the words. As the poem ends, Lucy is still; Shakespeare has moved to another place, an area upstage, with lighting to look like a different room. There, he sits at a table and writes.

6b) At Lucy's House: Entrance of the Fair Youth: 3:00

The Fair Youth breaks into the end of the song with a flourish, an athletic solo. The Fair Youth both likes the women of Lucy's brothel and is like them; he dances with them as a "client" and also as one of them. He is youthfully ebullient and playful, wild. The solo is interspersed with small dances of the Fair Youth with several of Lucy's women. At the end of the solo, Shakespeare, who has been writing in "the other room," stands. The ensemble exits, leaving only Lucy, the Fair Youth and Shakespeare on the stage. Shakespeare take the Fair Youth's hand and they exit, leaving Lucy onstage alone.

7)*Lucy "solo" with cast: the story of Lucy: 6:00

In which we know Lucy better; memories of the past: a montage of scenes that show us how Lucy became who/what she is—scenes that depict Lucy as a younger woman, how she came to be a prostitute, her survival as a prostitute and finally her taking of power, as well as she can in the world in which she lives, by owning her own house.
The emotions run the gamut but we understand that she is unbreakable, a survivor: she figures it out.

Mood: this is in her "monologue light" that will return later; moonlight, memory, blue

*This is an abridged version of the full libretto segment for this "scene"

11) Duet of Lucy and Shakes: 4:00

Lucy and Shakespeare dance an erotic, tense duet.
Emotions/mood: love and fear, approach/avoidance. He adores her in private but not in public. Near the end, or within the music, we hear as a call and response:

"Lucy, Lucy where you been?"
Living in brown sugar sin.
"Lucy, Lucy where's you man?"
He come and taste me when he can.

"Lucy, Lucy ain't you hitched?"

No, I'm just his so good bitch.

"Lucy, Lucy. Baby is you blue?"

Tch. I'm tired of feeling blackgirl used.

"Lucy, Lucy, that's no kinda life."

Black girl ain't no kinda wife.

"Lucy, Lucy, how you stand it?"

It's better than bein' empty handed.

"Lucy, Lucy, even you's God's flesh."

This world ain't wanna see that yet.

12) Solo of Shakespeare– he explains Lucy watches, Sonnet 141: 3:00

Shakespeare attempts to explain himself. Use Sonnet 141 as inspiration:

Mood/emotions: anxious, melancholy.
After this danced monologue, he takes her in his arms again.

13) Lucy solo: furious: 3:00

Lucy is furious. She pushes him violently away; maybe she strips in front of him (not completely) at the end. And then walks out.

16) Shakespeare solo with FY and full cast mirrors: 3:00

We see Shakespeare's angst, confusion and melancholy. The Fair Youth dances a solo in counterpoint to Shakespeare, a metaphoric mirror, while the full casts works in tableau with the hand held mirrors.

17) Trio of Shakespeare, Lucy and Fair Youth: 5:00

Pivotal moment: In which there is struggle and testing and tension between the three. A rotating "driver" in the movement, or the control point of a triangle. Eventually the tension, the defenses, become less, the characters and the movement become vulnerable, real, and thus calm and then harmonious. The tense triangle they've been in becomes a straight line.

Mood: coming out of darkness

18)*Dreaming is a Truth ballet: 7:00-8:00

Full cast: a formal dance that reflects that which was established the previous trio: resolution, harmony, love, joy, transformation, balance. Equality.

The principal trio participates for part of this, during which the men "fold into" Lucy and then the three disappear into the darkness.

*This is an abridged version of the full libretto segment for this "scene"

Epilogue: 2:00

A minimal solo for Lucy, mostly walking, but some movement interspersed. As the poem progresses, both Caroline and Rhiannon join Kayla on center stage. As they do this, she moves around and between them.
We hear Rhiannon's voice singing the Lucy theme. Then we hear the words:

This exiat sayeth that
We are fit for the degree of them that use us.
This exiat sayeth that
Lucy is burning. Think of her burning loose light wax and wick and
brown skin sweat slicked. See the room where he paid to know her.
Where he paid to, paid to, paid to know her. A rat in the room and a
velvet stage gown gone to seed.
This exiat sayeth that
Mick. Bob. Bowie. All my favorite rock stars have black babies.
This exiat sayeth that
Lucy got hot fire. I am fit for her degree if she can use me. More fire.
More fire and lick shot.
I am wild, and that I live by it, and that I like it; like the money, and the
witness, and the grotesque, and the yes, yes.
This exiat sayeth that
I am not a partridge, or a ruby. I am a potato, a beetroot. Not a
precious bird or jewel, but a dirt-dug tube. Rustle me, rub me all over,
and I will muddle your interiors with flecks of brown earth. You will
sigh at your soiled hands and then you will put them in your pockets to
pay for it.
This exiat sayeth that
You will come again to scour my body with your worthy, emolient
palm creases because I am that round, strange, colored victual...
and further, this examinate sayeth that you will dirt grit your nails
to gather me up and by God we will both be sustained. By God if you
warm and eat me, I will nourish and fatten you.

Lastly, at the lights fade, we hear Rhiannon singing the Lucy theme again.

photos

Owen Thorne, Kayla Rowser

Kayla Rowser, Paul Vasterling, Owen Thorne

Owen Thorne, Kayla Rowser

103

Brett Sjoblom, Kayla Rowser, Paul Vasterling, background: Francesco Turrisi

104

Brett Sjoblom, Owen Thorne

Owen Thorne, Kayla Rowser

Kayla Rowser

Kayla Rowser, Owen Thorne

Rhiannon Giddens

Rhiannon Giddens, Francesco Turrisi

Kayla Rowser, Paul Vasterling, Mollie Sansone, Brett Sjoblom, Owen Thorne

Kayla Rowser, Rhiannon Giddens, Caroline Randall Williams

Rhiannon Giddens, Paul Vasterling, Caroline Randall Williams
Photo by Alexandria Kominsky

Paul Vasterling

Paul Vasterling, Caroline Randall Williams
Photo by Alexandria Kominsky

Caroline Randall Williams

ACKNOWLEDGEMENTS

Some of these poems have appeared, in these or other versions, in the following journals:

The Iowa Review:
{For I have sworn thee fair}
{My love is as a fever longing still}
{Thy black is fairest in my judgment's place}
{And so the general of hot desire was, sleeping, by a virgin hand disarm'd.}
{But, love, hate on, for now I know thy mind}

Palimpsest: A Journal on Women, Gender, and the Black International:
In March
Nude Study
Gravy
Backbone.

Dr. Duncan Salkeld's indispensable hand helped in both bringing the historical Black Luce to light and guiding me to meet her. Tremendous thanks is also owed to Peter Richards, the steward of my undergraduate passage into the world of poetry, and to Derrick Harriell, Beth Anne Fennelly, Anne Fisher-Wirth, Chiyuma Elliott, and Rachel Eliza Griffiths, whose further guidance helped me bring the poems in this book from pen to paper to page.

I am grateful to the Cave Canem workshop for hearing Lucy's voice before I could, and to my mother Alice Randall, for hearing my voice before I could.

Ampersand Books gave Lucy her first space on the shelf. That will always be a priceless gift.

Paul Vasterling, this edition would not exist without your vision. Kayla Rowser, this edition would not exist without you being exactly you. Rhiannon Giddens, you are helping me to hear my own words the way I dreamed them.

Thank you also to Chet Weise for seeing the value in doing a good thing twice.

The following is a list of letters. The little list means a great deal to me, in that it represents people who mean a great deal more. STC, ELB, VKH, ARK, MM, TC and KL. Each of you has helped me in some way to carry Lucy into the light.

And of course, thank you to Shakespeare, and maybe even more importantly to Black Luce, for blazing a memory with enough space to imagine story.

– CRW

Photo by Caroline Allison

ABOUT THE POET

Caroline Randall Williams is a poet, fiction writer, essayist and educator in Nashville, Tennessee. She is co-author of the Phyllis Wheatley Award-winning young adult novel *The Diary of B.B. Bright*, and the NAACP Image Award-winning cookbook and memoir *Soul Food Love*. The Cave Canem fellow has been published in multiple journals, essay collections and news outlets, including The *Iowa Review, The Massachusetts Review, Southern Living, Gravy,* and the *New York Time*s. *Lucy Negro, Redux* is her debut poetry collection.

kept a brothell howse thys xpiall dwellt wt Cast
a gr̃ter of a yere Cast was a bawde to hyr owne
wyffe and wolde byd hyr goo vp to knavs to play
the harlott wt them and gett monye :/

She sayeth that Marye Dornelley had a sylke gowne
and was therabused and kept especially for by gentlemen
and welthye men wt velvett gaskens and such apparell
and not for the comen sorte :/

And Blacke Anes of Clerkenwell did agree wt
Cast and hys wyffe that when Blacke Anes had
any gret geste that thys xpiall or such other wemen
as Cast had sholde goo to them to Anes howse
and weir Marye Dornelleys gownes And Anes
Baynham sholde have thone halfe of the monye
and Cast thother halfe of the rest, Thys xpiall
went twise to Blacke Anes And there at those tyme
a yerk a straung of the ambassadors howse in fletstret
had thuse of hir bodye Anes had then halfe and Cast
wyffe had halfe of the rest She were then many
Dornelleys gownes and albert :/

One nyght ther was ij straungers yerk came to Cast
and one lay wt Marye Dornelley thother wt thys
xpiall the yerk gave eyther of them to Cast vjs and
to Marie and thys xpiall vs apiece / wherof Cast
had ij s apiece besides :/

A lytle after the same straunger came thether agay
and he that before had to doe wt Marie had to doe
wt thys xpiall and soe thother wt Marie :/

Also she sayeth that one mr Clarke a gentillman dwellett
in the cuntry lyenge at in Croked alley brought thys
xpiall from Croked whir she dwellt, vnto Cast and
ther he had often thuse of hir bodye And gave hir many
thinge nowe and then vjs :/

She sayeth that ther came so many yerk and knavs
thether to Cast to commytt whoredome ther that it is n
possible to tell howe manye they are :/

Also she confessyth, that wm meken brought many
men most cuntry men drovears and others vnto Cast
to abuse Marie Dornelley and other harlotts meken
had moch monye for his labo / Marie had some tome
to doe vij tymes in a daye wt sundry knaves :/